For information on all our
publications see
www.cap-ox.co.uk

THE CHILTERNS

A Little Souvenir

CHRIS ANDREWS PUBLICATIONS

Oilseed rape fields near Goring

THE CHILTERNS

Introduction

Designated as an Area of Outstanding Natural Beauty in 1965, the Chilterns lie only a short distance to the north-west of London yet remain an unspoilt region of chalk uplands, ancient woodlands, fertile valleys and quiet streams. Pleasing brick-and-flint villages complement the landscape. This book takes the reader on a photographic tour of the southern part of the Chilterns, that which lies between the Tring Gap in the north and the River Thames in the south.

Amidst this largely rural domain are numerous towns, each with its claims to fame and fragments of history. For example, Berkhamsted, where William the Conqueror accepted the surrender of the Saxons, has the remains of an important Norman castle. Over in the next valley to the south, Chesham used to be noted for the four 'B's of boots, brushes, beer and Baptists! The, effectively, twin towns of Amersham offer great contrast, with the original settlement in the valley and a classic example of

Latimer, near Chesham 5

6   A fine single-span bridge crosses the Thames at Reading

Metroland up on the hill, stimulated by the arrival of the railway in the late 19th century. Similarly, Beaconsfield has adjacent quarters that reflect the development of different modes of transport. The world's oldest - and many would say best - model village of Bekonscot is located there. A few miles to the west, and also on the old coach route to Oxford, lies High Wycombe, the largest town in the region. It used to be the centre of Britain's furniture industry, which still features in the town's economy. Nearby is Hughenden Manor, the home of former Prime Minister Benjamin Disraeli, now a major National Trust site.

View between Turville and Fingest   7

Henley-on-Thames

Chiltern villages offer a variety of styles and settings that put them alongside the best that other parts of the country can boast. Chalfont St Giles is a good example of the village pond-and-green layout, and masqueraded as Warmington-on-Sea when used as a location for the film 'Dad's Army'. Hambleden, tucked away in a side valley about a mile from the River Thames, enjoys a matchless setting surrounded by steep Chiltern slopes. Fingest is famous for St Bartholomew's, a

10 Market Hall, Old Amersham, built 1682

small church of great architectural interest. As its name suggests, Great Missenden is near the source of the River Mis; the Misbourne valley is particularly lovely. In 2005, the Roald Dahl Museum and Story Centre opened in the village. Cookham, on the Thames just east of Marlow, was the home of artist Stanley Spencer, who captured the beauty of the river there.

Over to the west, and running from south-west to north-east, the Chiltern escarpment rises dramatically from the Vale of Aylesbury, spring-line villages nestling at the foot of the slope. Whiteleaf Cross is visible for miles, cut into the chalk above the town of Princes Risborough. A little way to the north, Coombe Hill hosts an impressive monument to those who died in the Boer War.

So the Chilterns stand ready to provide the short-break seeker and holidaymaker with an accessible alternative to overseas destinations. Those who choose to explore its riches will not be disappointed.

12 Louisa Cottages, Tring, built 1893-1901, with the Rothschild Zoological Museum behind

Ivinghoe Beacon   13

14   Berkhamsted Castle, begun in 1066

Berkhamsted School, founded 1541   15

16   Grand Union Canal, Berkhamsted

Berkhamsted's 16th-century court house   17

18   Cottages on the south-western edge of Chesham

The Bury Manor, Chesham   19

20 Interior of St Mary's Church, Chesham and the new Clock Tower in the Market Place

St Mary's spire seen through autumn colours from Lowndes Park   21

22   Chenies Manor, built in approximately 1460. Chess Valley.

Shardeloes Lake, near Amersham, in winter   23

Old Amersham, set deep in the Misbourne Valley

26   St Mary's Church, Amersham, seen from the Memorial Gardens

Architectural variety in Old Amersham High Street   27

28   The large village of Great Missenden nestles in the upper Misbourne Valley

Missenden Abbey and The Roald Dahl Museum and Story Centre in Great Missenden   29

30   Chalfont St Giles village centre

The village pond, Chalfont St Giles   31

32   The White Hart, Beaconsfield

Poppies and oilseed rape near the town 33

34 The church of St Mary & All Saints, Beaconsfield

The War Memorial, Beaconsfield 35

36 The Thames at Cookham, home of artist Sidney Spencer

Cookham village pub   37

Aerial view of West Wycombe, with St Lawrence's Church on the right   39

View across fields to Fingest

42 St Bartholomew's church, Fingest, with its unusual tower

44   The village of Turville, much featured in 'The Vicar of Dibley'

Marlow

46   Hambleden, situated near the Thames between Marlow and Henley

Evening lights at Henley-on-Thames   47

48   Stonor Park and the House, north of Henley

Mapledurham Mill, with characteristic brick-and-flint wall on the right   49

50 Goring and Streatley, separated by the Thames and surrounded by the Chiltern Hills

The historic town of Wallingford seen from the castle ruins 51

52   The Ridgeway Path, seen here near Wallingford, runs along the Chiltern escarpment

Looking towards Ewelme. Jerome K Jerome is buried in the churchyard 53

54 **The town of Watlington seen from Watlington Hill**

Watlington Town Hall (detail) 55

56 St Andrew's church, Chinnor

Princes Risborough. Risborough means a hill where brushwood grows   57

58   The Market Hall, Princes Risborough

St Mary's Church, Princes Risborough 59

60 Whiteleaf Cross, above Princes Risborough, and Coombe Hill monument

A cottage at Monks Risborough, with distinctive herring-bone brick pattern   61

62 Looking down Wendover High Street

Timber frame thatched cottages in Wendover   63

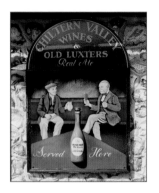

First published 2007 by Chris Andrews Publications
15 Curtis Yard North Hinksey Lane Oxford OX2 0LX
Telephone: +44(0)1865 723404 **www.cap-ox.com**
Photos: Chris Andrews, Colin Nutt, Mike Brain, Ian Meredith, Bill Reynolds, Gary Matthews, Andrew Baskott
Text: Colin Nutt © Chris Andrews Publications
ISBN 978-1905385-69-0

Front Cover: Turville Title page: The Ridgeway This page: Chiltern valley Winery Back cover: Bisham

The Chilterns

This endpaper shows
the south of the area
pictured in this book.
The endpaper at the
front of the book
shows the northern
area covered.

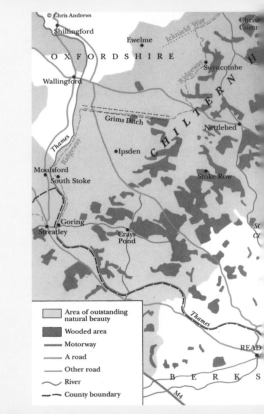